Published in 2008 by Concordia Publishing House
Text © 1993 Concordia Publishing House
3558 S. Jefferson Avenue
St. Louis, MO 63118-3968
1-800-325-3040 • www.cph.org

Illustrations © 2008 by Concordia Publishing House

Manufactured in China

1 2 3 4 5 6 7 8 9 10   17 16 15 14 13 12 11 10 09 08

The Easter Day Surprise

Story by Jane L. Fryar
Art by Michelle Dorenkamp

CONCORDIA PUBLISHING HOUSE • SAINT LOUIS

The sky above hung black as ink,
While very low a hint of pink
Began to tint the eastern sky,
To light three crosses standing by.

In heaven, God the Father said,
"My Son has risen from the dead.
He died to pay the price for sin.
I've brought Him back to life again.

"So now, My angels, rise and go
To earth so that His friends all know
That Jesus lives. They need not cry.
He lives again, no more to die."

Like lightning bolts two angels sped
At once to do what God had said,
While joy and praise began to rise
At God's great Easter Day surprise.

A squad of soldiers, strong and brave,
Stood guard around the Savior's grave.
They felt the earth begin to quake
And roll, and quake some more, and shake.

That wasn't all! An angel bright
Eclipsed the early morning light.
The soldiers fell. They rose to run
Just at the rising of the sun.

The stone that shut the tomb up tight
Was no match for the angel's might.
He rolled it back. The door stood wide.
But Jesus did not lie inside.

When Mary came out to the tomb,
Her heart felt numb with grief and gloom.
She saw the stone there, rolled away,
And knew that she could not delay.

At once she hurried back to tell
Two other friends, who ran pell-mell
Out to the tomb, themselves to see
Just what this mystery could be.

John got there first; then Peter came.
Both puzzled over who to blame.
Christ's body had just disappeared!
His tomb stood empty, as they'd feared.

They shrugged, then walked back into town,
Their faces long, their eyes turned down.
But Mary stayed alone to try
To find the Savior, and to cry.

The garden silent, Mary wept.
Were Jesus' promises not kept?
Why had He died? She didn't know.
She only knew she'd loved Him so.

His tomb stood empty . . . No, look there—
Two angels sent to show God's care!
But Mary didn't even blink.
Her grief had made it hard to think.

Then as she turned around to leave,
A soft voice asked, "Why do you grieve?
Why all these tears?" Then Mary said,
"I know for sure my Lord is dead.

"If you're the gardener, please sir, how
Can I find Him? Tell me right now,
And I will carry Him away.
If you know where He is, please say."

Then Jesus spoke a single word—
Just "Mary," but she knew she'd heard
Her Savior's voice. It dried her tears
And wiped away her many fears.

She shouted, "Teacher!" Jesus smiled
And said, "It's true. I'm here, My child.
I died and then I rose again.
Now you are free from death and sin.

"Go, now! You can believe your eyes.
Go, share My Easter Day surprise.
Go, let your Easter laughter ring.
Go, tell My friends. Shout, praise, and sing!"

Jesus came and said to them, "All authority in heaven and on earth has been given to Me. Go therefore and make disciples of all nations, baptizing them in the name of the Father and of the Son and of the Holy Spirit, teaching them to observe all that I have commanded you. And behold, I am with you always, to the end of the age."

Matthew 28:18–20